No Time to Cook™

Speedy Chicken

READY TO SERVE IN 30 MINUTES OR LESS

Publications International, Ltd.

Pictured on the front cover: Broiled Chicken with Honeyed Onion Sauce *(page 78)*.

Pictured on the back cover: Quick Chicken Pot Pie *(page 88)*.

ISBN: 0-7853-1980-8

Manufactured in U.S.A.

8   7   6   5   4   3   2   1

Nutritional Analysis: In the case of multiple choices, the first ingredient, the lowest amount and the lowest serving yield are used to calculate the nutritional analysis. "Serve with" suggestions are not included unless otherwise stated.

Microwave Cooking: Microwave ovens vary in wattage. The microwave cooking times given in this publication are approximate. Use the cooking times as guidelines and check for doneness before adding more time. Consult manufacturer's instructions for suitable microwave-safe cooking dishes.

Speedy Chicken

CONTENTS

KITCHEN

WHAT'S YOUR SPEED, WHAT'S YOUR NEED?

The recipes in this publication are divided into four categories. These classifications, noted under the title of each recipe, are as follows:

PANTRY COOKING

The ultimate convenience: No-Stop Shopping! Whip up these delicious recipes in 30 minutes or less with ingredients already on hand in your kitchen.

20 MINUTES OR LESS

Great taste in no time! These fuss-free dishes are a snap to prepare in 20 minutes or less with a little help from convenience foods.

6 INGREDIENTS OR LESS

See just how much flavor can come from so few ingredients (not including salt, pepper or water)! Ready to serve in 30 minutes or less, these simple recipes will keep your shopping time and your cooking time to a minimum.

MAKE–AHEAD RECIPE

Prepare these mouthwatering dishes when you have the time . . . then enjoy them even more when you don't! Cook according to your schedule—hours, days or even several weeks ahead of time—so a fresh, homemade dish can still be savored on those extra-busy days.

WHAT'S THE TIME?

Each recipe includes a "prep and cook" time. These times are based on the approximate amount of time needed to assemble and prepare ingredients prior to cooking and the minimum amount of time required to cook, broil, microwave or chill the foods in the recipe. These recipes have been developed for the most efficient use of your time. Some preparation steps are completed before the cooking begins, while others are done during the cooking time.

CHICKEN BASICS

Shopping Tips for Chicken

• Check the package for the U.S.D.A. Grade A rating; chicken in most supermarkets should be government inspected. Look for secure, unbroken packaging, as well as "sell-by" date stamp that indicates the last day the chicken should be sold.

• Physically inspect the chicken before purchasing. Its skin should be creamy white to deep yellow; meat should never look gray or pasty. Odors could signal spoilage.

Proper Chicken Storage

• Fresh, raw chicken can be stored in its original wrap for up to two days in the coldest part of the refrigerator. However, freeze chicken immediately if you do not plan to use it within two days after purchasing.

• Buying boneless skinless chicken breasts in large quantities saves both time and money—but don't let those savings go to waste. Separate the breasts into meal-sized portions, wrap tightly in plastic wrap and store them in a labeled, dated resealable plastic storage bag.

• Thaw frozen chicken, wrapped, in the refrigerator for best results. Never thaw chicken on the kitchen counter; this promotes bacterial growth.

Handling Chicken

• When handling raw chicken, keep everything that comes in contact with it clean. Raw chicken should be rinsed and patted dry with paper towels before cooking; cutting boards and knives must be washed in hot sudsy water after using and hands must be scrubbed thoroughly before and after handling.

• Raw chicken can harbor harmful salmonella bacteria. If bacteria is transferred to work surfaces, utensils or hands, they could contaminate other foods as well as the cooked chicken and cause food poisoning. With careful handling and proper cooking, this is easily prevented.

• Chicken should always be cooked completely before eating. You should never cook chicken partially, then store it to be finished later, since this promotes bacterial growth as well.

• Boneless chicken pieces are done when the centers are no longer pink.

Speedy Soups

Pozole

1 large onion, thinly sliced
1 tablespoon olive oil
2 teaspoons dried oregano leaves
1 clove garlic, minced
½ teaspoon ground cumin
2 cans (about 14 ounces each) chicken broth
1 package (10 ounces) frozen corn
1 to 2 cans (4 ounces each) chopped green chilies, undrained
1 can (2¼ ounces) sliced black olives, drained
¾ pound boneless skinless chicken breasts

1 Combine onion, oil, oregano, garlic and cumin in Dutch oven. Cover and cook over medium heat about 6 minutes or until onion is tender, stirring occasionally.

2 Stir chicken broth, corn, chilies and olives into onion mixture. Cover and bring to a boil over high heat.

3 While soup is cooking, cut chicken into thin strips. Add to soup. Reduce heat to medium-low; cover and cook 3 to 4 minutes or until chicken is cooked through.

Makes 6 servings

Prep and cook time: 20 minutes

For a special touch, sprinkle Pozole with chopped fresh cilantro before serving.

Nutrients per serving: Calories: 193, Total Fat: 8 g, Protein: 16 g, Carbohydrate: 15 g, Cholesterol: 41 mg, Sodium: 990 mg, Dietary Fiber: 3 g

Dietary Exchanges: Vegetable: 1, Bread: ½, Meat: 1½, Fat: 1

Mexicali Chicken Stew

1 package (1.25 ounces)
    taco seasoning,
    divided
12 ounces boneless
    skinless chicken
    thighs
2 cans (14½ ounces
    each) stewed
    tomatoes with
    onions, celery and
    green peppers
1 package (9 ounces)
    frozen green beans
1 package (10 ounces)
    frozen corn
4 cups tortilla chips

1 Place half of taco seasoning in small bowl. Cut chicken thighs into 1-inch pieces; coat with taco seasoning.

2 Coat large nonstick skillet with nonstick cooking spray. Cook and stir chicken 5 minutes over medium heat. Add tomatoes, beans, corn and remaining taco seasoning; bring to a boil. Reduce heat to medium-low; simmer 10 minutes. Top with tortilla chips before serving.

Makes 4 servings

Prep and cook time: 20 minutes

Serving suggestion: Whip up nachos in a flash to serve along with the stew. Spread some of the tortilla chips on a plate; dot with salsa and sprinkle with cheese. Heat just until cheese is melted.

Nutrients per serving: Calories: 396, Total Fat: 13 g, Protein: 20 g, Carbohydrate: 52 g, Cholesterol: 47 mg, Sodium: 955 mg, Dietary Fiber: 5 g

Dietary Exchanges: Vegetable: 3, Bread: 2, Meat: 2, Fat: 1½

Apple and Chicken Soup

1 sweet potato
(8 ounces)
1 tablespoon olive oil
2 ribs celery, thinly sliced
½ medium onion, chopped
1 teaspoon dried thyme
leaves
½ teaspoon dried
rosemary
¼ teaspoon dried sage
leaves
¼ teaspoon ground
nutmeg
2 cans (about 14 ounces
each) chicken broth
1 cup apple juice
1 large Golden Delicious
or McIntosh apple,
peeled and chopped
⅔ cup uncooked small
pasta shells
¾ pound boneless
skinless chicken
breast

1 Prick sweet potato in several places with fork. Microwave on HIGH 6 to 8 minutes or until almost tender; set aside. (Sweet potato will finish cooking and become tender as it stands.)

2 While sweet potato is cooking, heat oil in 3-quart saucepan over medium-high heat. Add celery, onion, thyme, rosemary, sage and nutmeg; cook, covered, 3 to 4 minutes or until onion is tender. Add chicken broth, juice and apple. Bring to a boil over high heat; stir in pasta. Reduce heat to medium-high; boil, uncovered, 8 to 10 minutes.

3 Cut chicken into ¼-inch-wide strips. Pull skin from sweet potato; cut into 1-inch pieces. Add chicken and sweet potato to soup. Reduce heat to medium; simmer 3 to 5 minutes or until chicken is no longer pink in center and pasta is tender. Ladle into bowls.

Makes 4 to 6 servings

Prep and cook time: 25 minutes

Serving suggestion: Serve with wedges of warm herb-cheese bread.

Nutrients per serving: Calories: 330, Total Fat: 8 g, Protein: 24 g, Carbohydrate: 40 g, Cholesterol: 68 mg, Sodium: 969 mg, Dietary Fiber: 2 g
Dietary Exchanges: Fruit: 1, Bread: 1½, Meat: 2½, Fat: ½

Bounty Soup

½ pound yellow
  crookneck squash
2 cups frozen mixed
  vegetables
1 teaspoon dried parsley
  flakes
⅛ teaspoon dried
  rosemary
⅛ teaspoon dried thyme
  leaves
⅛ teaspoon salt
⅛ teaspoon black pepper
2 teaspoons vegetable oil
3 boneless skinless
  chicken breast
  halves (about ¾
  pound), chopped
1 can (about 14 ounces)
  fat-free reduced-
  sodium chicken broth
1 can (14½ ounces)
  stewed tomatoes,
  undrained

1 Cut wide part of squash in half lengthwise, lay flat and cut crosswise into ¼-inch slices. Place squash, mixed vegetables, parsley, rosemary, thyme, salt and pepper in medium bowl.

2 Heat oil in large saucepan over medium-high heat. Add chicken; stir-fry 2 minutes. Stir in vegetables and seasonings. Add chicken broth and tomatoes with liquid, breaking up large tomatoes. Cover; bring to a boil. Reduce heat to low. Cover; cook 5 minutes or until vegetables are tender. *Makes 4 servings*

Prep and cook time: 30 minutes

Serving suggestion: Serve soup with grilled mozzarella cheese sandwiches.

Nutrients per serving: Calories: 238, Total Fat: 6 g, Protein: 25 g, Carbohydrate: 21 g, Cholesterol: 52 mg, Sodium: 557 mg, Dietary Fiber: 3 g

Dietary Exchanges: Vegetable: 4, Meat: 2½

Country Chicken Chowder

1 pound chicken tenders
2 tablespoons margarine
   or butter
1 small onion, chopped
1 rib celery, sliced
1 small carrot, sliced
1 can (10¾ ounces)
   cream of potato soup
1 cup milk
1 cup frozen corn
½ teaspoon dried dill
   weed

1 Cut chicken tenders into ½-inch pieces.

2 Melt margarine in large saucepan or Dutch oven over medium-high heat. Add chicken; cook and stir 5 minutes.

3 Add onion, celery and carrot; cook and stir 3 minutes. Stir in soup, milk, corn and dill; reduce heat to low. Cook about 8 minutes or until corn is tender and chowder is heated through. Add salt and pepper to taste. *Makes 4 servings*

Prep and cook time: 27 minutes

Nutrients per serving: Calories: 310, Total Fat: 11 g, Protein: 30 g, Carbohydrate: 22 g, Cholesterol: 77 mg, Sodium: 781 mg, Dietary Fiber: 2 g

Dietary Exchanges: Vegetable: 1, Bread: 1, Meat: 3, Fat: 1

Cook's Notes

Chowder was originally associated with seafood but now is used to describe any kind of thick, chunky soup that is made with milk and potatoes.

Thai Noodle Soup

1 package (3 ounces)
   ramen noodles
¾ pound chicken tenders
2 cans (about 14 ounces
   each) chicken broth
¼ cup shredded carrot
¼ cup frozen snow peas
2 tablespoons thinly
   sliced green onion
   tops
½ teaspoon bottled
   minced garlic
¼ teaspoon ground ginger
3 tablespoons chopped
   cilantro
½ lime, cut into 4 wedges

1 Break up noodles into smaller pieces. Cook noodles according to package directions, discarding flavor packet. Drain; set aside.

2 Cut chicken tenders into ½-inch pieces. Combine chicken broth and chicken tenders in large saucepan or Dutch oven; bring to a boil over medium heat. Cook 2 minutes.

3 Add carrots, snow peas, green onions, garlic and ginger. Reduce heat to low; simmer 3 minutes. Add cooked noodles and cilantro; heat through. Serve soup with lime wedges. *Makes 4 servings*

Prep and cook time: 15 minutes

Nutrients per serving: Calories: 200, Total Fat: 7 g, Protein: 23 g, Carbohydrate: 13 g, Cholesterol: 78 mg, Sodium: 1,148 mg, Dietary Fiber: 2 g
Dietary Exchanges: Bread: 1, Meat: 3

BLT Chicken Salad for Two

2 boneless skinless
    chicken breast
    halves
¼ cup mayonnaise or
    salad dressing
½ teaspoon black pepper
4 large leaf lettuce
    leaves
1 large tomato, seeded
    and diced
3 slices crisp-cooked
    bacon, crumbled
1 hard-cooked egg, sliced

1 Brush chicken with mayonnaise; sprinkle with pepper. Grill over hot coals 5 to 7 minutes on each side or until no longer pink in center. Cut into thin strips. Refrigerate up to 2 days.

2 To complete recipe, arrange lettuce leaves on serving plates. Top with chicken, tomato, bacon and egg.

Makes 2 servings

Make-ahead time: up to 2 days before serving
Final prep time: 5 minutes

Serving suggestion: Spoon additional mayonnaise or salad dressing over top of salad.

Nutrients per serving: Calories: 444, Total Fat: 34 g, Protein: 32 g, Carbohydrate: 4 g, Cholesterol: 194 mg, Sodium: 390 mg, Dietary Fiber: 1 g

Dietary Exchanges: Vegetable: 1, Meat: 4, Fat: 4

Chicken Stir-Fry Salad with Peanut Dressing

PEANUT DRESSING
 ½ cup chicken broth
 ½ cup smooth peanut
   butter
 2 tablespoons molasses
   or brown sugar
 2 tablespoons lime or
   lemon juice
 1 tablespoon soy sauce
 ¼ teaspoon ground red
   pepper
 ⅛ teaspoon garlic powder

SALAD
 1 pound chicken tenders,
   cut into ½-inch
   pieces
 ¼ teaspoon salt
 2 tablespoons vegetable
   oil
 1 package (16 ounces)
   frozen broccoli,
   carrots and water
   chestnuts blend
 2 tablespoons soy sauce
 1 package (10 ounces)
   ready-to-eat salad
   greens*
 ¼ cup dry-roasted
   peanuts

Hot cooked rice can be substituted for salad greens.

1 To prepare Peanut Dressing, microwave chicken broth on HIGH until hot, about 30 seconds. Place in blender with remaining dressing ingredients; process about 15 seconds or until well blended. Set aside.

2 Sprinkle chicken with salt. Heat oil in wok or large skillet over medium-high heat until hot. Add chicken; stir-fry 3 minutes or until chicken begins to brown.

3 Add frozen vegetables. Reduce heat to medium. Cover and cook 5 minutes more or until vegetables are crisp-tender, stirring occasionally. Stir in soy sauce. Remove from heat.

4 Arrange salad greens on plates; top with chicken mixture. Sprinkle with peanuts. Serve with Peanut Dressing. *Makes 4 servings*

Prep and cook time: 20 minutes

Nutrients per serving: Calories: 521, Total Fat: 31 g, Protein: 38 g, Carbohydrate: 27 g, Cholesterol: 70 mg, Sodium: 1,322 mg, Dietary Fiber: 4 g
Dietary Exchanges: Vegetable: 2, Bread: 1, Meat: 4, Fat: 4

Gazebo Chicken

4 boneless chicken
  breast halves (about
  1½ pounds)
6 cups torn butter lettuce
  leaves or mixed baby
  greens
1 ripe cantaloupe, seeded
  and cut into
  12 wedges
1 large carrot, shredded
½ cup (3 ounces) fresh
  raspberries
⅔ cup honey-mustard
  salad dressing,
  divided

1 Preheat broiler. Place chicken, skin side down, on broiler pan coated with nonstick cooking spray. Season with salt and pepper to taste. Broil 4 to 5 inches from heat source 8 minutes. Turn; sprinkle with salt and pepper. Broil 6 to 8 minutes or until chicken is no longer pink in center. Remove to cutting board; cool.

2 Place lettuce on large serving platter; arrange cantaloupe and carrot around lettuce.

3 Slice each chicken breast diagonally into fourths; place over lettuce.

4 Arrange raspberries over salad; drizzle with 2 tablespoons dressing. Serve with remaining dressing.
Makes 4 servings

Prep and cook time: 25 minutes

Serving suggestion: Serve salad with corn muffins and herb-flavored butter.

Nutrients per serving: Calories: 465, Total Fat: 21 g, Protein: 40 g, Carbohydrate: 29 g, Cholesterol: 103 mg, Sodium: 332 mg, Dietary Fiber: 3 g
Dietary Exchanges: Fruit: 2, Meat: 4, Fat: 2

Mediterranean Chicken Salad

1 box (5¼ ounces) quick-
    cooking bulgur wheat
¾ pound chicken tenders
1 tablespoon olive oil
1 cup chopped tomato
1 cup chopped fresh
    parsley
2 green onions, sliced
2 tablespoons lemon
    juice

1 Prepare bulgur according to package directions; set aside.

2 While bulgur is cooking, cut chicken tenders into 1-inch chunks. Heat olive oil in medium skillet. Add chicken; cook and stir 4 to 5 minutes or until no longer pink in center. Remove from heat; cool slightly.

3 Combine cooked bulgur, chicken, tomato, parsley, green onions and lemon juice in large bowl; toss gently to blend. Season with salt and pepper to taste.

Makes 4 servings

Prep and cook time: 20 minutes

Tip: For quick-chopped parsley, snip ends of rinsed and dried parsley with scissors.

Nutrients per serving: Calories: 277, Total Fat: 6 g, Protein: 24 g, Carbohydrate: 32 g, Cholesterol: 52 mg, Sodium: 64 mg, Dietary Fiber: 9 g
Dietary Exchanges: Bread: 2, Meat: 2½

Cobb Salad

1 package (10 ounces) torn mixed salad greens *or* 8 cups torn romaine lettuce
½ pound deli chicken, cut ¼ inch thick
1 large tomato, seeded and chopped
⅓ cup bacon bits or crumbled crisply cooked bacon
1 large ripe avocado, diced
⅓ cup blue cheese or Caesar salad dressing

1 Place lettuce in large serving bowl.

2 Dice chicken; place in center of lettuce.

3 Arrange tomato, bacon and avocado in rows on either side of chicken.

4 Drizzle portion of dressing over salad. Serve immediately with remaining dressing.

Makes 4 servings

Prep time: 15 minutes

Nutrients per serving: Calories: 204, Total Fat: 12 g, Protein: 13 g, Carbohydrate: 11 g, Cholesterol: 28 mg, Sodium: 957 mg, Dietary Fiber: 4 g

Dietary Exchanges: Vegetable: 2, Meat: 1½, Fat: 1½

Serve It With Style!

*S*erve this colorful salad with warm French bread and pound cake with fresh fruit for dessert.

Grilled Chicken and Melon Salad

¾ **cup orange marmalade, divided**

¼ **cup plus 2 tablespoons white wine vinegar, divided**

2 tablespoons low-sodium soy sauce

1 tablespoon grated fresh ginger

4 boneless skinless chicken breast halves

½ **cantaloupe, peeled, seeded and sliced**

½ **honeydew melon, peeled, seeded and cut into 1-inch-thick slices**

2 tablespoons olive oil

2 tablespoons minced fresh cilantro

1 teaspoon jalapeño pepper sauce

10 cups mixed lettuce greens

1 pint fresh strawberries, halved

1 Combine ⅓ cup orange marmalade, 2 tablespoons vinegar, soy sauce and ginger. Brush marmalade mixture over chicken and melons. Arrange melons in grill basket or thread onto skewers.

2 Grill chicken over hot coals 5 to 7 minutes on each side or until no longer pink in center. Grill melons, covered, 2 to 3 minutes on each side. Refrigerate overnight.

3 Combine remaining marmalade, ¼ cup vinegar, oil, cilantro and jalapeño pepper sauce in jar with tight-fitting lid; shake well to blend. Refrigerate.

4 To complete recipe, arrange lettuce, chicken, melons and strawberries on serving plates; spoon marmalade mixture over top.   *Makes 4 servings*

Make-ahead time: up to 1 day before serving
Final prep time: 5 minutes

For a special touch, garnish with fresh produce such as red and green bell peppers or jalapeño peppers.

Nutrients per serving: Calories: 498, Total Fat: 11 g, Protein: 31 g, Carbohydrate: 78 g, Cholesterol: 69 mg, Sodium: 395 mg, Dietary Fiber: 9 g

Dietary Exchanges: Fruit: 5, Vegetable: 1, Meat: 3

Lemon Chicken and Rice Salad

2 tablespoons olive oil
1½ pounds chicken
    tenders, cut into bite-
    size pieces
⅓ cup lemon juice
1 teaspoon dried thyme
    leaves
½ teaspoon salt
½ teaspoon black pepper
1 can (about 14 ounces)
    fat-free reduced-
    sodium chicken broth
2 cups uncooked instant
    brown rice
4 cups ready-to-use fresh
    spinach, torn into
    bite-size pieces
2 medium red apples, cut
    into ½-inch-thick
    slices
1 tablespoon dried
    parsley flakes
⅓ cup honey-Dijon salad
    dressing

1 Heat oil in large skillet over medium-high heat. Add chicken; cook until slightly browned. Add lemon juice, thyme, salt and pepper. Cover; reduce heat to medium and cook 8 to 10 minutes or until chicken is no longer pink in center. Remove from heat and cool.

2 Bring chicken broth to a boil in medium saucepan over medium-high heat. Add rice; cover, reduce heat to low and cook 10 minutes or until chicken broth is absorbed. Remove from heat and cool.

3 Combine spinach, rice, chicken and apples in large bowl. Sprinkle with parsley flakes. Pour salad dressing over top; toss to combine. *Makes 6 servings*

Prep and cook time: 30 minutes

Serving suggestion: Serve with fresh green and red grapes and toasted sourdough bread slices.

For a special touch, garnish with a fresh thyme sprig.

Nutrients per serving: Calories: 438, Total Fat: 14 g, Protein: 22 g, Carbohydrate: 60 g, Cholesterol: 38 mg, Sodium: 420 mg, Dietary Fiber: 6 g

Dietary Exchanges: Fruit: ½, Vegetable: 1, Bread: 3, Meat: 2, Fat: 1

6 INGREDIENTS OR LESS

Chicken-Pesto Pizza

8 ounces chicken tenders
1 medium onion, thinly
   sliced
⅓ cup prepared pesto
3 medium plum
   tomatoes, thinly
   sliced
1 (14-inch) prepared
   pizza crust
1 cup (4 ounces)
   shredded mozzarella
   cheese

1 Preheat oven to 450°F. Cut chicken tenders into bite-size pieces. Coat medium nonstick skillet with nonstick cooking spray; cook and stir chicken over medium heat 2 minutes. Add onion and pesto; cook and stir about 3 minutes or until chicken is cooked through.

2 Arrange tomato slices and chicken mixture on pizza crust to within 1 inch of edge. Sprinkle cheese over topping. Bake 8 minutes or until pizza is hot and cheese is melted and bubbly.   *Makes 6 servings*

Prep and cook time: 22 minutes

Nutrients per serving: Calories: 427, Total Fat: 14 g, Protein: 22 g, Carbohydrate: 51 g, Cholesterol: 36 mg, Sodium: 831 mg, Dietary Fiber: 4 g

Dietary Exchanges: Vegetable: 1, Bread: 3, Meat: 1½, Fat: 2½

Broiled Chicken, Avocado and Papaya Sandwich

½ cup teriyaki sauce
¼ cup honey
2 teaspoons olive oil
1 pound boneless
  skinless chicken
  breasts
1 loaf (16 ounces)
  sourdough bread
1 large avocado, sliced
1 medium papaya, peeled
  and sliced
1 medium tomato, sliced
⅓ cup ranch salad
  dressing
½ cup cashews, chopped

1 Combine teriyaki sauce, honey and oil in medium bowl; whisk to combine. Reserve ¼ cup marinade. Add chicken to remaining marinade, turning to coat well. Cover with plastic wrap; refrigerate at least 1 hour, turning chicken occasionally.

2 Preheat broiler. Remove chicken from marinade; discard marinade. Place chicken on broiler pan coated with nonstick cooking spray. Broil 4 to 5 inches from heat source 6 to 8 minutes per side or until chicken is no longer pink in center, brushing occasionally with reserved ¼ cup marinade. Set aside; cool. Cut chicken into ½-inch-thick slices. Cover and refrigerate.

3 To complete recipe, cut sourdough bread in half lengthwise. Hollow out inside of bread halves, leaving ¼-inch shell. Discard extra bread.

4 Layer chicken on bottom of bread shell. Top with avocado, papaya and tomato. Drizzle ranch dressing over top and sprinkle with cashews. Cover with bread shell top. Press down firmly and cut into slices.

Makes 6 servings

Make-ahead time: up to 1 day before serving
Final prep time: 10 minutes

Serving suggestion: Serve with fresh fruit such as cantaloupe and raspberries.

Nutrients per serving: Calories: 539, Total Fat: 20 g, Protein: 27 g, Carbohydrate: 64 g, Cholesterol: 49 mg, Sodium: 903 mg, Dietary Fiber: 4 g
Dietary Exchanges: Fruit: 2, Bread: 2, Meat: 3, Fat: 2½

Stir-Fry Pita Sandwiches

12 ounces chicken tenders
1 onion, thinly sliced
1 red bell pepper, cut into strips
½ cup zesty Italian dressing
¼ teaspoon red pepper flakes
4 pita bread rounds
8 leaves leaf lettuce
4 tablespoons crumbled feta cheese

1 Cut chicken tenders in half lengthwise and crosswise. Coat large nonstick skillet with nonstick cooking spray. Cook and stir chicken over medium heat 3 minutes. Add onion and bell pepper; cook and stir 2 minutes. Add Italian dressing and red pepper flakes; cover and cook 3 minutes. Remove from heat; uncover and let cool 5 minutes.

2 While chicken cools, cut pita breads in half to form pockets. Line each pocket with lettuce leaf. Spoon chicken filling into pockets; sprinkle with feta cheese.

Makes 4 servings

Prep and cook time: 17 minutes

Nutrients per serving: Calories: 536, Total Fat: 28 g, Protein: 30 g, Carbohydrate: 46 g, Cholesterol: 85 mg, Sodium: 1,029 mg, Dietary Fiber: 6 g

Dietary Exchanges: Vegetable: 2, Bread: 2½, Meat: 2½, Fat: 4

CUTTING CORNERS Salad dressings can offer a surprising amount of time-saving convenience in the kitchen. Their basic components of oil, vinegar, herbs and spices provide a ready-made marinade or seasoned oil for cooking meats and poultry. There's no need to fumble in the pantry for a lot of separate ingredients—they're already together in one bottle.

Mustard-Glazed Chicken Sandwiches

½ cup honey-mustard
    barbecue sauce,
    divided
4 Kaiser rolls, split
4 boneless skinless
    chicken breast halves
    (about 1 pound)
4 slices Swiss cheese
4 leaves leaf lettuce
8 slices tomato

1 Spread about 1 teaspoon barbecue sauce on cut sides of each roll.

2 Pound chicken breast halves between 2 pieces of plastic wrap to ½-inch thickness with flat side of meat mallet or rolling pin. Spread remaining barbecue sauce over chicken.

3 Cook chicken in large nonstick skillet over medium-low heat 5 minutes per side or until no longer pink in center. Remove skillet from heat. Place cheese slices on chicken; let stand 3 minutes to melt.

4 Place lettuce leaves and tomato slices on roll bottoms; top with chicken and roll tops.

Makes 4 servings

Prep and cook time: 19 minutes

Serving suggestion: Serve sandwiches with yellow tomatoes, baby carrots and celery sticks.

Nutrients per serving: Calories: 464, Total Fat: 14 g, Protein: 39 g, Carbohydrate: 43 g, Cholesterol: 95 mg, Sodium: 787 mg, Dietary Fiber: trace
Dietary Exchanges: Bread: 3, Meat: 4, Fat: ½

Tortilla "Pizza"

1 can (10 ounces) chunk white chicken in water, drained
1 can (14½ ounces) Mexican-style stewed tomatoes, drained
1 green onion, minced
2 teaspoons cumin, divided
½ teaspoon garlic powder
1 cup fat-free refried beans
¼ cup chopped fresh cilantro, divided
2 large or 4 small flour tortillas
1 cup (4 ounces) shredded Monterey Jack cheese

1 Preheat broiler. Combine chicken and tomatoes in medium bowl. Add green onion, 1 teaspoon cumin and garlic powder. Mix well; set aside.

2 Mix refried beans, remaining 1 teaspoon cumin and 2 tablespoons cilantro in small bowl; set aside.

3 Place tortillas on baking sheet. Broil 30 seconds to 1 minute per side or until crisp but not browned. Remove from oven. *Decrease oven temperature to 400°F.* Spread each tortilla evenly with bean mixture. Spoon chicken mixture over beans; top with cheese. Bake 5 minutes.

4 *Reset oven temperature to broil.* Broil tortillas 2 to 3 minutes or until cheese melts. **Do not let tortilla edges burn.** Remove from oven; top with remaining 2 tablespoons cilantro. Serve immediately. (If using large tortillas, cut each in half.)   *Makes 4 servings*

Prep and cook time: 19 minutes

Serving suggestion: serve with a green salad tossed with avocado slices along with a lemon vinaigrette dressing.

Nutrients per serving: Calories: 344, Total Fat: 12 g, Protein: 30 g, Carbohydrate: 29 g, Cholesterol: 30 mg, Sodium: 916 mg, Dietary Fiber: 2 g
Dietary Exchanges: Vegetable: 1, Bread: 1½, Meat: 3, Fat: ½

Reuben Chicken Melts

4 boneless skinless
   chicken breast
   halves
1 large onion, cut into
   ½-inch slices
1¼ cups Thousand Island
   salad dressing,
   divided
2 cups shredded red
   cabbage
1½ cups (6 ounces)
   shredded Swiss
   cheese
4 French rolls, split

1 Brush chicken and onion with ½ cup salad dressing; set aside.

2 Combine ¼ cup salad dressing and cabbage; mix well. Set aside.

3 Grill chicken over hot coals 5 to 7 minutes on each side or until no longer pink in center. Sprinkle chicken evenly with Swiss cheese during last minute of grilling. Grill onion 4 to 5 minutes on each side or until browned and tender. Grill rolls until toasted.

4 Spread toasted sides of rolls with remaining ½ cup salad dressing. Place chicken on roll bottoms. Top with onion, cabbage mixture and roll tops. Serve immediately. *Makes 4 servings*

Prep and cook time: 25 minutes

Nutrients per serving: Calories: 720, Total Fat: 44 g, Protein: 42 g, Carbohydrate: 38 g, Cholesterol: 132 mg, Sodium: 957 mg, Dietary Fiber: 4 g

Dietary Exchanges: Vegetable: 1, Bread: 2, Meat: 4, Fat: 7

Open-Faced Chicken Sandwiches with Broiled Vegetables

1 small red onion, cut into ¼-inch slices
1 package (8 ounces) sliced portobello mushrooms
1 cup Italian salad dressing
4 boneless skinless chicken breast halves (about 1½ pounds)
4 slices whole grain bread
4 leaves leaf lettuce
1 cup avocado, cut into ½-inch cubes
¼ cup bacon bits

1 Preheat broiler.

2 Dip onion and mushroom slices in Italian dressing; set aside.

3 Pound chicken breast halves between 2 pieces of plastic wrap to ½-inch thickness with flat side of meat mallet or rolling pin. Dip chicken in remaining Italian dressing.

4 Place chicken on broiler pan; broil 4 to 5 inches from heat source 4 minutes per side or until no longer pink in center. Broil onion and mushrooms with chicken during last 4 minutes of cooking time.

5 Top bread slices with lettuce leaves, chicken, mushrooms, onions, avocado and bacon bits.

Makes 4 servings

Prep and cook time: 20 minutes

Cook's Note: Place 1 slice Monterey Jack cheese on top of avocado and return sandwich to broiler until cheese is melted. Sprinkle bacon bits over cheese.

Nutrients per serving: Calories: 685, Total Fat: 45 g, Protein: 46 g, Carbohydrate: 28 g, Cholesterol: 104 mg, Sodium: 855 mg, Dietary Fiber: 3 g

Dietary Exchanges: Vegetable: 1, Bread: 1, Meat: 4½, Fat: 7½

Provençal Chicken Sandwiches

½ pound sliced deli
chicken breast, cut
into ½-inch-wide
strips
½ cup sliced roasted red
peppers
½ cup sliced red onion
¼ cup sliced pitted ripe
olives
1 tablespoon extra-virgin
olive oil
1 tablespoon red wine
vinegar
½ teaspoon salt
¼ teaspoon black pepper
Fresh parsley
4 submarine or hoagie
sandwich rolls

1 Combine chicken, roasted peppers, onion and olives in medium bowl.

2 Whisk together oil, vinegar, salt and black pepper in small bowl. Pour over chicken mixture; toss until coated. Cover and refrigerate at least 1 hour or up to 2 days.

3 To complete recipe, chop enough parsley to measure 2 tablespoons. Stir into chicken mixture. Cut rolls in half; fill with chicken mixture. Serve immediately.

Makes 4 servings

Make-ahead time: at least 1 hour or up to 2 days before serving
Final prep time: 5 minutes

Nutrients per serving: Calories: 528, Total Fat: 11 g, Protein: 25 g, Carbohydrate: 82 g, Cholesterol: 47 mg, Sodium: 1,884 mg, Dietary Fiber: 5 g

Dietary Exchanges: Vegetable: ½, Bread: 5, Meat: 2, Fat: 1

LIGHTEN UP

To reduce sodium, substitute ½ pound sliced, cooked boneless skinless chicken breasts for deli chicken.

◆

20 MINUTES OR LESS

Chicken and Tomatoes in Red Pepper Cream

9 ounces refrigerated
angel hair pasta
1 jar (7 ounces) roasted
red peppers, drained
⅓ cup half-and-half
2 teaspoons Dijon
mustard
1 teaspoon salt
12 sun-dried tomatoes
(packed in oil),
drained
1 tablespoon olive oil
4 boneless skinless
chicken breast
halves (about
1 pound)
Grated Parmesan
cheese

1 Cook pasta according to package directions; drain.

2 While the pasta is cooking, combine red peppers, half-and-half, mustard and salt in food processor or blender; cover and process until smooth. Set aside.

3 Rinse tomatoes in warm water; drain and pat dry. Cut in half.

4 Heat olive oil in large skillet over medium-high heat. Add chicken; cook, uncovered, 5 to 6 minutes per side.

5 Add tomatoes and red pepper mixture. Simmer 3 minutes or until sauce thickens slightly and chicken is no longer pink in center. Season to taste with black pepper.

6 Serve chicken and sauce over pasta. Sprinkle with Parmesan cheese. *Makes 4 servings*

Prep and cook time: 19 minutes

Nutrients per serving: Calories: 542, Total Fat: 17 g, Protein: 37 g, Carbohydrate: 62 g, Cholesterol: 75 mg, Sodium: 782 mg, Dietary Fiber: 1 g

Dietary Exchanges: Vegetable: 1, Bread: 3½, Meat: 3½, Fat: 1½

Chicken Marengo

8 ounces uncooked rotini
1 tablespoon olive oil or
    vegetable oil
1 pound boneless
    skinless chicken
    breasts, cut into
    1-inch pieces
3 small onions, each cut
    into 6 wedges
2 cloves garlic, minced
1 tablespoon all-purpose
    flour
1 cup chicken broth
¾ cup dry white wine
¼ cup tomato paste
4 ounces small
    mushrooms
2 (3×1-inch) strips
    orange peel
½ teaspoon dried thyme
    leaves
½ teaspoon dried tarragon
    leaves

1 Cook pasta according to package directions; drain.

2 While pasta is cooking, heat oil in large saucepan over medium-high heat. Add chicken, onions and garlic; cook 5 minutes or until chicken is browned. Stir in flour; cook over medium heat 1 minute, stirring constantly.

3 Stir in chicken broth, wine, tomato paste, mushrooms, orange peel, thyme and tarragon; bring to a boil. Reduce heat to low; simmer, covered, 10 minutes or until chicken is tender. Season to taste with salt and pepper. Serve over pasta.

Makes 4 (1-cup) servings

Prep and cook time: 30 minutes

Nutrients per serving: Calories: 417, Total Fat: 9 g, Protein: 34 g, Carbohydrate: 43 g, Cholesterol: 113 mg, Sodium: 451 mg, Dietary Fiber: 4 g
Dietary Exchanges: Vegetable: 2, Bread: 2, Meat: 3

KITCHEN HOW-TO

To remove 3×1-inch strips of orange peel, use a vegetable peeler. Be careful to remove the colored portion of the skin only; the white pith has a bitter taste.

Peppy Pesto Toss

8 ounces uncooked ziti or mostaccioli
1 package (16 ounces) frozen bell pepper and onion strips, thawed
½ pound deli chicken breast or smoked chicken breast, cut ½ inch thick
1 cup half-and-half
½ cup pesto sauce
¼ cup grated Parmesan or Asiago cheese

1 Cook pasta according to package directions.

2 Add pepper and onion mixture to pasta water during last 2 minutes of cooking. Meanwhile, cut chicken into ½-inch cubes.

3 Drain pasta and vegetables in colander.

4 Combine half-and-half, pesto and chicken in saucepan used to prepare pasta. Cook 2 minutes or until heated through. Return pasta and vegetables to saucepan; toss well.

5 Sprinkle with cheese. Serve immediately.

Makes 4 servings

Prep and cook time: 20 minutes

Nutrients per serving: Calories: 581, Total Fat: 26 g, Protein: 28 g, Carbohydrate: 60 g, Cholesterol: 75 mg, Sodium: 1,040 mg, Dietary Fiber: 2 g
Dietary Exchanges: Vegetable: 3, Bread: 3, Meat: 2, Fat: 4

Herbed Chicken over Spinach Fettuccine

10 ounces uncooked
    spinach fettuccine
1 tablespoon olive oil
8 boneless skinless
    chicken thighs (1¼
    pounds), cut into
    1-inch pieces
1½ teaspoons dried
    oregano leaves
1½ teaspoons dried thyme
    leaves
1 cup dry white wine
1 teaspoon chicken
    bouillon granules
    Pinch sugar
2 tablespoons cold
    butter, cut into small
    pieces

1 Cook pasta according to package directions; drain.

2 While pasta is cooking, heat oil in large nonstick skillet over medium heat. Add chicken, oregano and thyme; cook 3 minutes. Remove chicken with slotted spoon; cover to keep warm.

3 Add wine, ½ cup water, bouillon and sugar to skillet; bring to a boil over high heat, scraping particles from bottom of skillet. Boil 2 minutes or until liquid is reduced by half. Gradually stir butter into simmering sauce.

4 Serve chicken over pasta; spoon sauce over chicken and pasta.   *Makes 4 servings*

Prep and cook time: 20 minutes

Nutrients per serving: Calories: 513, Total Fat: 22 g, Protein: 32 g, Carbohydrate: 39 g, Cholesterol: 159 mg, Sodium: 425 mg, Dietary Fiber: 0 g

Dietary Exchanges: Bread: 2½, Meat: 3½, Fat: 3

Creamy Chicken Florentine

8 ounces uncooked fusilli
1 box (10 ounces) frozen
    chopped spinach
1 package (8 ounces)
    cream cheese
½ cup chicken broth
½ teaspoon dried Italian
    seasoning
¼ teaspoon salt
¼ teaspoon black pepper
    Dash hot pepper sauce
1 can (10 ounces)
    premium chunk white
    chicken in water,
    drained
1 tablespoon lemon juice

1 Cook pasta according to package directions; drain.

2 While pasta is cooking, remove outer wrapping from spinach, leaving spinach in box. Microwave spinach on HIGH 3 minutes or until thawed. Drain in colander; cool slightly. Squeeze spinach to remove excess moisture. Set aside.

3 Combine cream cheese, chicken broth, Italian seasoning, salt, black pepper and hot pepper sauce in microwavable 2-quart casserole. Cover and microwave on HIGH 2 to 3 minutes; whisk until smooth and blended.

4 Add spinach, chicken and lemon juice. Microwave on HIGH 2 to 3 minutes or until hot, stirring after 1 minute.

5 Combine pasta and spinach mixture in large bowl; toss until blended. *Makes 4 servings*

Prep and cook time: 20 minutes

Nutrients per serving: Calories: 523, Total Fat: 22 g, Protein: 32 g, Carbohydrate: 52 g, Cholesterol: 64 mg, Sodium: 698 mg, Dietary Fiber: 2 g

Dietary Exchanges: Vegetable: 1, Bread: 3, Meat: 3, Fat: 2½

Braised Chicken with Artichokes

1 jar (4 ounces)
    marinated artichoke
    hearts, undrained
1 jar (2 ounces) chopped
    pimiento, drained
⅔ cup white wine
3 tablespoons honey
    mustard
¼ teaspoon salt
¼ teaspoon pepper
8 ounces uncooked wide
    egg noodles
¾ cup herb-seasoned
    stuffing mix, crushed
4 boneless skinless
    chicken breast
    halves (4 ounces
    each)
1 tablespoon olive oil
2 tablespoons chopped
    fresh parsley

1 Drain artichoke marinade into small skillet. Set artichokes aside in bowl.

2 Add pimiento, wine, mustard, salt and pepper to small skillet; bring to a boil. Cook over high heat 3 minutes. Pour mixture over artichokes; refrigerate, covered, at least 45 minutes.

3 To complete recipe, cook noodles according to package directions; drain.

4 While noodles are cooking, place stuffing in large resealable plastic food storage bag. Add chicken; seal bag and toss to coat chicken.

5 Heat oil in large skillet over medium-high heat until hot. Remove chicken from bag; shake off excess stuffing. Cook chicken 3 minutes per side or until browned. Add artichoke mixture. Bring to a boil. Reduce heat to low. Simmer, covered, 10 minutes or until chicken is no longer pink in center.

6 Serve chicken mixture over noodles; sprinkle with parsley.   *Makes 4 servings*

Make-ahead time: at least 1 hour or up to 3 hours before serving
Final prep and cook time: 22 minutes

Nutrients per serving: Calories: 471, Total Fat: 9 g, Protein: 35 g, Carbohydrate: 54 g, Cholesterol: 118 mg, Sodium: 544 mg, Dietary Fiber: 1 g
Dietary Exchanges: Vegetable: 2, Bread: 3, Meat: 3

Super Speedy Chicken on Angel Hair Pasta

1 package (12 ounces)
   angel hair pasta
3 boneless skinless
   chicken breast
   halves (12 ounces)
2 cups baby carrots
1 tablespoon olive oil
2 cups broccoli florets
1 teaspoon chicken
   bouillon granules
1 jar (28 ounces) chunky-
   style pasta sauce
⅓ cup grated Parmesan
   cheese

1 Cook pasta according to package directions; drain.

2 While pasta is cooking, cut chicken into 1-inch cubes. Cut carrots in half lengthwise.

3 Heat oil in large nonstick skillet over medium heat. Add chicken; cook and stir 5 minutes. Stir in carrots, broccoli, ¼ cup water and chicken bouillon. Reduce heat to low; cover and cook 5 minutes or until vegetables are crisp-tender.

4 Bring pasta sauce to a boil in medium saucepan over high heat. Place pasta on plates; top with hot pasta sauce and chicken and vegetable mixture. Sprinkle with cheese.   *Makes 6 servings*

Prep and cook time: 25 minutes

Nutrients per serving: Calories: 448, Total Fat: 9 g, Protein: 26 g, Carbohydrate: 66 g, Cholesterol: 39 mg, Sodium: 799 mg, Dietary Fiber: 2 g

Dietary Exchanges: Vegetable: 1, Bread: 4, Meat: 1½, Fat: 1

Chicken Tetrazzini with Roasted Red Peppers

6 ounces uncooked egg
   noodles
3 tablespoons margarine
   or butter
¼ cup all-purpose flour
1 can (about 14 ounces)
   chicken broth
1 cup whipping cream
2 tablespoons dry sherry
2 cans (6 ounces each)
   sliced mushrooms,
   drained
1 jar (7½ ounces)
   roasted red peppers,
   cut into ½-inch strips
2 cups chopped cooked
   chicken
1 teaspoon Italian
   seasoning
½ cup grated Parmesan
   cheese

1 Cook noodles according to package directions; drain.

2 While noodles are cooking, melt margarine in medium saucepan over medium heat. Add flour and whisk until smooth. Add chicken broth; bring to a boil over high heat. Remove from heat. Gradually add whipping cream and sherry; stir to combine.

3 Combine mushrooms, red peppers and noodles in large bowl; toss to combine. Add half the chicken broth mixture to noodle mixture. Combine remaining chicken broth mixture, chicken and Italian seasoning in large bowl.

4 Spoon noodle mixture into serving dish. Make a well in center of noodles and spoon in chicken mixture. Sprinkle with cheese. *Makes 6 servings*

Prep and cook time: 20 minutes

Nutrients per serving: Calories: 452, Total Fat: 25 g, Protein: 23 g, Carbohydrate: 33 g, Cholesterol: 125 mg, Sodium: 1,017 mg, Dietary Fiber: 2 g

Dietary Exchanges: Vegetable: 1, Bread: 2, Meat: 2, Fat: 4

Grilled Rosemary Chicken

2 tablespoons lemon
   juice
2 tablespoons olive oil
2 cloves garlic, minced
2 tablespoons minced
   fresh rosemary
¼ teaspoon salt
4 boneless skinless
   chicken breasts

1 Whisk together lemon juice, oil, garlic, rosemary and salt in small bowl. Pour into shallow glass dish. Add chicken, turning to coat both sides with lemon juice mixture. Cover and marinate in refrigerator 15 minutes, turning chicken once.

2 Grill chicken over medium-hot coals 5 to 6 minutes per side or until chicken is no longer pink in center.

Makes 4 servings

Prep and cook time: 30 minutes

Nutrients per serving: Calories: 156, Total Fat: 5 g, Protein: 25 g, Carbohydrate: trace, Cholesterol: 69 mg, Sodium: 104 mg, Dietary Fiber: trace
Dietary Exchanges: Meat: 3

Cook's Notes

For added flavor, moisten a few sprigs of fresh rosemary and toss on the hot coals just before grilling.

Chicken Tostadas

6 (8-inch) flour tortillas
1 can (15 ounces) black
  beans, rinsed and
  drained
2 teaspoons chili powder,
  divided
1 teaspoon ground
  cumin, divided
½ cup hot salsa
12 ounces chicken tenders
2 cups finely chopped
  tomatoes, drained
1 cup chopped onion
1½ cups (6 ounces)
  shredded Cheddar
  cheese
2 cups shredded Romaine
  or iceberg lettuce

1 Preheat oven to 350°F. Place tortillas on two large baking sheets, overlapping as little as possible. Spray both sides of tortillas with nonstick cooking spray. Bake 7 minutes. Turn tortillas over and bake 3 minutes more or until no longer soft and flexible.

2 While tortillas are baking, place beans in food processor and process until smooth. Transfer to medium saucepan. Stir in 1 teaspoon chili powder, ½ teaspoon cumin and salsa; bring to a boil over medium heat.

3 Cut chicken into ½-inch pieces. Sprinkle with remaining 1 teaspoon chili powder and remaining ½ teaspoon cumin. Coat large nonstick skillet with cooking spray; heat over medium heat. Add chicken; cook and stir 5 minutes or until cooked through.

4 Spread bean mixture on tortillas to within ½ inch of edges. Top with chicken, tomatoes, onion and cheese. Bake 2 minutes or just until cheese is melted. Top with lettuce; serve immediately. *Makes 6 servings*

Prep and cook time: 28 minutes

For a special touch, top each tostada with a dollop of sour cream.

Nutrients per serving: Calories: 379, Total Fat: 14 g, Protein: 30 g, Carbohydrate: 39 g, Cholesterol: 65 mg, Sodium: 599 mg, Dietary Fiber: 7 g
Dietary Exchanges: Vegetable: 2, Bread: 2, Meat: 2½, Fat: 1

Easy Chicken Couscous

2 tablespoons olive oil
1 onion, chopped
1 pound chicken tenders
1½ cups quick-cooking
    couscous
½ teaspoon salt
1 can (14½ ounces)
    diced tomatoes with
    roasted garlic,
    undrained
1 can (15½ ounces)
    chick-peas, drained
    and rinsed
¼ teaspoon ground
    cinnamon
¼ teaspoon ground cumin
1 cup frozen peas
¼ teaspoon hot pepper
    sauce

1 Heat oil in large skillet over medium-high heat. Add onion; cook and stir 3 minutes or until translucent. Add chicken tenders; cook and stir 5 minutes.

2 While chicken is cooking, bring 2½ cups water to a boil in medium saucepan. Add couscous and salt; cover and remove from heat. Let stand 10 minutes.

3 While couscous is standing, add tomatoes, chick-peas, cinnamon and cumin to chicken mixture; mix well. Reduce heat to medium-low. Cover and cook 5 minutes, stirring occasionally. Add peas and hot pepper sauce. Cover and cook 5 minutes more or until chicken is no longer pink in center.

4 Fluff couscous with fork. Serve chicken mixture with couscous. *Makes 6 servings*

Prep and cook time: 25 minutes

Nutrients per serving: Calories: 394, Total Fat: 13 g, Protein: 28 g, Carbohydrate: 40 g, Cholesterol: 51 mg, Sodium: 652 mg, Dietary Fiber: 9 g

Dietary Exchanges: Vegetable: 2, Bread: 2, Meat: 2½, Fat: 1½

Chicken in Mushroom Sauce

2 cups uncooked instant
    white rice
2 tablespoons olive oil
4 boneless skinless
    chicken breast
    halves (1 pound)
1 cup sliced mushrooms
1 small onion, thinly
    sliced
1 teaspoon bottled
    minced garlic
1 can (10¾ ounces)
    cream of mushroom
    soup

1 Cook rice according to package directions.

2 While rice is cooking, heat oil in large nonstick skillet over medium heat. Cook chicken 3 to 4 minutes per side or until lightly browned. Remove chicken; set aside.

3 Add mushrooms, onion and garlic to skillet. Cook 1 minute, stirring constantly. Reduce heat to low; stir in soup and pepper to taste. Add chicken and cook about 7 minutes or until chicken is no longer pink in center. Serve over rice. *Makes 4 servings*

Prep and cook time: 25 minutes

Nutrients per serving: Calories: 467, Total Fat: 16 g, Protein: 31 g, Carbohydrate: 49 g, Cholesterol: 70 mg, Sodium: 681 mg, Dietary Fiber: 2 g

Dietary Exchanges: Vegetable: 1, Bread: 3, Meat: 3, Fat: 1½

LIGHTEN UP

An easy way to reduce fat and sodium is to simply substitute 1 can ⅓-less-salt 99% fat-free cream of mushroom soup.

◆

Glazed Chicken & Vegetable Skewers

GOLDEN GLAZE
    ¼ cup apricot or peach
        preserves
    2 tablespoons spicy
        brown mustard
    2 cloves garlic, minced

CHICKEN & VEGETABLE SKEWERS
    12 small red or new
        potatoes
    1 pound boneless
        skinless chicken
        thighs or breasts, cut
        into 1-inch pieces
    1 yellow or red bell
        pepper, cut into
        1-inch pieces
    ½ small red onion, cut
        into 1-inch pieces

1 For glaze, combine preserves, mustard and garlic in small bowl; mix well. Transfer to container with tight-fitting lid. Store in refrigerator up to 2 weeks.

2 To complete recipe, prepare barbecue grill for direct cooking.

3 Place potatoes in large saucepan; cover with water. Bring to a boil over high heat. Cook 10 minutes or until almost tender. Rinse under cool water; drain.

4 Alternately thread chicken, potatoes, bell pepper and onion onto skewers. Brush glaze evenly over both sides.

5 Place skewers on grid over medium-hot coals. Grill, on covered grill, 14 minutes for chicken breasts or 16 minutes for chicken thighs or until chicken is no longer pink in center and vegetables are crisp-tender, turning once. *Makes 4 servings*

Make-ahead time: up to 2 weeks before serving
Final prep and cook time: 14 to 16 minutes

Serving suggestion: Serve skewers with a spinach salad.

Nutrients per serving: Calories: 272, Total Fat: 6 g, Protein: 16 g, Carbohydrate: 39 g, Cholesterol: 46 mg, Sodium: 153 mg, Dietary Fiber: trace
Dietary Exchanges: Fruit: 1, Bread: 1½, Meat: 2

Saucy Rice and Chicken Dinner

1 can (about 14 ounces) chicken broth
2 teaspoons seasoned salt, divided
3 cups instant whole grain brown rice
2 ribs celery, chopped
1 package (10 ounces) frozen peas
6 boneless skinless chicken breast halves (1½ pounds)
1 tablespoon olive oil
1 can (10¾ ounces) cream of chicken soup
½ cup milk
½ cup (2 ounces) shredded Cheddar cheese

1 Bring chicken broth, ½ cup water and 1 teaspoon seasoned salt to a boil in large saucepan over high heat. Stir in rice, celery and peas; reduce heat to medium-low. Cover and simmer 5 minutes. Remove from heat and let stand, covered, 5 minutes or until rice is tender.

2 Sprinkle remaining 1 teaspoon seasoned salt over chicken breasts. Heat oil in large skillet over medium heat. Add chicken; cook 5 minutes per side or until no longer pink in center.

3 Combine soup and milk in small saucepan; bring to a boil over medium-high heat.

4 Spoon rice mixture onto serving platter. Arrange chicken breasts over rice; top with soup mixture and sprinkle with cheese. *Makes 6 servings*

Prep and cook time: 26 minutes

Nutrients per serving: Calories: 405, Total Fat: 12 g, Protein: 35 g, Carbohydrate: 38 g, Cholesterol: 87 mg, Sodium: 1,307 mg, Dietary Fiber: 4 g

Dietary Exchanges: Vegetable: 1, Bread: 2, Meat: 4

Broiled Chicken with Honeyed Onion Sauce

2 pounds boneless skinless chicken thighs
4 teaspoons olive oil, divided
1 teaspoon salt, divided
1 teaspoon paprika
1 teaspoon dried oregano leaves
½ teaspoon ground cumin
¼ teaspoon black pepper
1 onion, sliced
2 cloves garlic, minced
¼ cup golden raisins
¼ cup honey
2 tablespoons lemon juice

1 Preheat broiler. Rub chicken with 2 teaspoons olive oil. Combine ½ teaspoon salt, paprika, oregano, cumin and pepper; rub mixture over chicken.

2 Place chicken on broiler pan. Broil about 6 inches from heat source 5 minutes per side or until chicken is no longer pink in center.

3 While chicken is cooking, heat remaining 2 teaspoons oil in medium nonstick skillet. Add onion and garlic; cook about 8 minutes or until onion is dark golden brown, stirring occasionally.

4 Stir in raisins, honey, lemon juice, ¼ cup water and remaining ½ teaspoon salt. Simmer, uncovered, until slightly thickened. Spoon sauce over chicken.

Makes 4 servings

Prep and cook time: 28 minutes

Serving Suggestion: Serve with a quick-cooking rice pilaf and mixed green salad.

Nutrients per serving: Calories: 434, Total Fat: 19 g, Protein: 35 g, Carbohydrate: 31 g, Cholesterol: 124 mg, Sodium: 653 mg, Dietary Fiber: 1 g
Dietary Exchanges: Fruit: 1½, Vegetable: 1, Meat: 5, Fat: 1

Chicken Primavera

4 boneless skinless
   chicken breast
   halves
3 tablespoons all-purpose
   flour
½ teaspoon dried basil
   leaves
¼ teaspoon salt
¼ teaspoon black
   pepper
1 package (16 ounces)
   frozen vegetable
   mixture (broccoli, red
   pepper, onion and
   mushroom
   combination)
4 teaspoons olive oil
2 cloves garlic, crushed
1 container (10 ounces)
   alfredo sauce

1 Pound chicken breasts between 2 pieces of plastic wrap to ½-inch thickness with flat side of meat mallet or rolling pin. Combine flour, basil, salt and pepper in resealable plastic food storage bag. Add chicken; seal bag and shake to coat evenly with flour mixture. Set aside.

2 Make small cut in frozen vegetable package. Microwave on HIGH 2 minutes; set aside.

3 Heat oil in large skillet over medium-high heat. Add garlic; cook and stir 1 minute. Add chicken; cook 3 minutes per side.

4 Reduce heat to medium. Add vegetable mixture to skillet. Cook, covered, 5 to 8 minutes or until chicken is no longer pink in center and vegetables are tender.

5 While chicken is cooking, heat alfredo sauce in medium saucepan or microwave oven according to package directions. Spoon sauce over each serving of chicken and vegetables. Serve immediately.

Makes 4 servings

Prep and cook time: 28 minutes

Serving suggestion: To complete the meal, serve with spaghetti, a tossed green salad and a fresh fruit tart for dessert.

Nutrients per serving: Calories: 466, Total: Fat 30 g, Protein: 31 g, Carbohydrate: 17 g, Cholesterol: 116 mg, Sodium: 538 mg, Dietary Fiber: 3 g
Dietary Exchanges: Milk: ½, Vegetable: 2, Meat: 3, Fat: 4½

Chicken Curry

½ cup uncooked white
rice
1 small onion
2 boneless skinless
chicken breast
halves
1 tablespoon margarine
or butter
1 clove garlic, minced
1 teaspoon curry powder
¼ teaspoon ground ginger
3 tablespoons raisins
1 cup coarsely chopped
apple, divided
1 teaspoon chicken
bouillon granules
¼ cup plain nonfat yogurt
2 teaspoons all-purpose
flour

1 Cook rice according to package directions.

2 While rice is cooking, cut onion into thin slices. Cut chicken into ¾-inch cubes.

3 Heat margarine, garlic, curry powder and ginger in medium skillet over medium heat. Add chicken; cook and stir 2 minutes. Add onion, raisins and ¾ cup chopped apple; cook and stir 3 minutes. Stir in chicken bouillon and ¼ cup water. Reduce heat to low; cover and cook 2 minutes.

4 Combine yogurt and flour in small bowl. Stir several tablespoons liquid from skillet into yogurt mixture. Stir yogurt mixture back into skillet. Cook and stir just until mixture starts to boil.

5 Serve chicken curry over rice; top with remaining ¼ cup chopped apple. *Makes 2 servings*

Prep and cook time: 28 minutes

For a special touch, sprinkle chicken with green onion slivers just before serving.

Nutrients per serving: Calories: 479, Total Fat: 10 g, Protein: 32 g, Carbohydrate: 66 g, Cholesterol: 85 mg, Sodium: 610 mg, Dietary Fiber: 4 g
Dietary Exchanges: Fruit: 2, Bread: 2½, Meat: 3

Chicken Cacciatore

8 ounces uncooked wide
   ribbon pasta
1 can (15 ounces)
   chunky Italian-style
   tomato sauce
1 cup chopped green bell
   pepper
1 cup sliced onion
1 cup sliced mushrooms
4 boneless skinless
   chicken breast
   halves (1 pound)

1 Cook pasta according to package directions; drain.

2 While pasta is cooking, combine tomato sauce, bell pepper, onion and mushrooms in microwavable dish. Cover loosely with plastic wrap or waxed paper; microwave on HIGH 6 to 8 minutes, stirring halfway through cooking time.

3 While sauce mixture is cooking, coat large skillet with nonstick cooking spray and heat over medium-high heat. Cook chicken breasts 3 to 4 minutes per side or until lightly browned.

4 Add sauce mixture to skillet; season with salt and pepper to taste. Reduce heat to medium and simmer 12 to 15 minutes. Serve over pasta.   *Makes 4 servings*

Prep and cook time: 30 minutes

Nutrients per serving: Calories: 392, Total Fat: 5 g, Protein: 35 g, Carbohydrate: 52 g, Cholesterol: 118 mg, Sodium: 633 mg, Dietary Fiber: 4 g

Dietary Exchanges: Bread: 2, Meat: 3

Honey-Citrus Chicken Breasts with Fruit Salsa

6 boneless chicken
    breast halves
    (1½ pounds)

MARINADE
⅓ cup honey
3 tablespoons olive oil
1 teaspoon grated lemon
    peel
1 teaspoon grated lime
    peel
Juice of 1 lemon
Juice of 1 lime
¾ teaspoon ground cumin
⅛ teaspoon ground red
    pepper or to taste

SALSA
1 orange
2 cups coarsely chopped
    fresh pineapple
½ cup orange juice
Juice of 1 lime
1 teaspoon grated lime
    peel
1 jalapeño pepper,
    seeded and minced
2 tablespoons chopped
    fresh cilantro

1 Place chicken in a large resealable plastic food storage bag. For marinade, combine honey, oil, lemon and lime peel, lemon and lime juices, cumin and ground red pepper in small bowl. Reserve 2 tablespoons marinade; pour remaining marinade over chicken. Seal bag and turn to coat. Marinate at least 1 hour or up to 24 hours in refrigerator, turning once or twice.

2 For salsa, grate 1 tablespoon orange peel; set aside. Peel orange and chop coarsely. Combine grated orange peel, chopped orange and remaining salsa ingredients except cilantro in medium bowl. Cover and refrigerate up to 24 hours.

3 To complete recipe, preheat broiler. Remove chicken from marinade and place on broiler pan coated with nonstick cooking spray; discard marinade. Broil about 6 inches from heat source 6 to 8 minutes per side or until chicken is no longer pink in center, basting with reserved 2 tablespoons marinade. While chicken is cooking, stir cilantro into salsa. Serve salsa over chicken.

Makes 6 servings

Make-ahead time: up to 24 hours before serving
Final prep and cook time: 10 minutes

Nutrients per serving: Calories: 224, Total Fat: 5 g, Protein: 26 g, Carbohydrate: 18 g, Cholesterol: 69 mg, Sodium: 72 mg, Dietary Fiber: 1 g
Dietary Exchanges: Fruit: 1, Meat: 3

Quick Chicken Pot Pie

1 pound boneless skinless chicken thighs

1 can (about 14 ounces) chicken broth

3 tablespoons all-purpose flour

2 tablespoons butter, softened

1 package (10 ounces) frozen mixed vegetables, thawed

1 can (about 4 ounces) button mushrooms, drained

¼ teaspoon dried basil leaves

¼ teaspoon dried oregano leaves

¼ teaspoon dried thyme leaves

1 cup biscuit baking mix

6 tablespoons milk

1 Cut chicken into 1-inch cubes. Place chicken and chicken broth in large skillet; cover and bring to a boil over high heat. Reduce heat to medium; simmer, uncovered, 5 minutes or until chicken is tender.

2 While chicken is cooking, mix flour and butter; set aside. Combine mixed vegetables, mushrooms, basil, oregano and thyme in 2-quart casserole dish.

3 Add flour mixture to chicken and chicken broth in skillet; stir with wire whisk until smooth. Cook and stir until thickened. Add to vegetable mixture; mix well. Cover and refrigerate up to 24 hours.

4 To complete recipe, preheat oven to 450°F. Blend biscuit mix and milk in medium bowl until smooth. Drop 4 scoops batter onto chicken mixture.

5 Bake 20 to 25 minutes or until biscuits are browned and casserole is hot and bubbly. *Makes 4 servings*

Make-ahead time: up to 1 day before serving
Final prep and cook time: 30 minutes

Nutrients per serving: Calories: 417, Total Fat: 19 g, Protein: 24 g, Carbohydrate: 36 g, Cholesterol: 87 mg, Sodium: 1,056 mg, Dietary Fiber: 3 g
Dietary Exchanges: Vegetable: 2, Bread: 1½, Meat: 2½, Fat: 2½

Chicken Breasts Smothered in Tomatoes and Mozzarella

4 boneless skinless chicken breast halves (about 1½ pounds)
3 tablespoons olive oil, divided
1 cup chopped onions
2 teaspoons bottled minced garlic
1 can (14½ ounces) Italian-style stewed tomatoes
1½ cups (6 ounces) shredded mozzarella cheese

1 Preheat broiler.

2 Pound chicken breasts between 2 pieces of plastic wrap to ¼-inch thickness using flat side of meat mallet or rolling pin.

3 Heat 2 tablespoons oil in ovenproof skillet over medium heat. Add chicken and cook 3 to 4 minutes per side or until no longer pink in center. Transfer to plate; cover and keep warm.

4 Heat remaining 1 tablespoon oil in same skillet over medium heat. Add onions and garlic; cook and stir 3 minutes. Add tomatoes; bring to a simmer. Return chicken to skillet, spooning tomato mixture over chicken.

5 Sprinkle cheese over top. Broil 4 to 5 inches from heat source until cheese is melted.   *Makes 4 servings*

Prep and cook time: 20 minutes

Nutrients per serving: Calories: 449, Total Fat: 21 g, Protein: 50 g, Carbohydrate: 12 g, Cholesterol: 127 mg, Sodium: 477 mg, Dietary Fiber: trace
Dietary Exchanges: Vegetable: 2, Meat: 6, Fat: 1½

Index

Recipe Category Index

METRIC CONVERSION CHART

VOLUME MEASUREMENTS (dry)

⅛ teaspoon = 0.5 mL
¼ teaspoon = 1 mL
½ teaspoon = 2 mL
¾ teaspoon = 4 mL
1 teaspoon = 5 mL
1 tablespoon = 15 mL
2 tablespoons = 30 mL
¼ cup = 60 mL
⅓ cup = 75 mL
½ cup = 125 mL
⅔ cup = 150 mL
¾ cup = 175 mL
1 cup = 250 mL
2 cups = 1 pint = 500 mL
3 cups = 750 mL
4 cups = 1 quart = 1 L

VOLUME MEASUREMENTS (fluid)

1 fluid ounce (2 tablespoons) = 30 mL
4 fluid ounces (½ cup) = 125 mL
8 fluid ounces (1 cup) = 250 mL
12 fluid ounces (1½ cups) = 375 mL
16 fluid ounces (2 cups) = 500 mL

WEIGHTS (mass)

½ ounce = 15 g
1 ounce = 30 g
3 ounces = 90 g
4 ounces = 120 g
8 ounces = 225 g
10 ounces = 285 g
12 ounces = 360 g
16 ounces = 1 pound = 450 g

DIMENSIONS

1/16 inch = 2 mm
⅛ inch = 3 mm
¼ inch = 6 mm
½ inch = 1.5 cm
¾ inch = 2 cm
1 inch = 2.5 cm

OVEN TEMPERATURES

250°F = 120°C
275°F = 140°C
300°F = 150°C
325°F = 160°C
350°F = 180°C
375°F = 190°C
400°F = 200°C
425°F = 220°C
450°F = 230°C

BAKING PAN SIZES

Utensil	Size in Inches/Quarts	Metric Volume	Size in Centimeters
Baking or Cake Pan (square or rectangular)	8×8×2	2 L	20×20×5
	9×9×2	2.5 L	22×22×5
	12×8×2	3 L	30×20×5
	13×9×2	3.5 L	33×23×5
Loaf Pan	8×4×3	1.5 L	20×10×7
	9×5×3	2 L	23×13×7
Round Layer Cake Pan	8×1½	1.2 L	20×4
	9×1½	1.5 L	23×4
Pie Plate	8×1¼	750 mL	20×3
	9×1¼	1 L	23×3
Baking Dish or Casserole	1 quart	1 L	—
	1½ quart	1.5 L	—
	2 quart	2 L	—